Jack's Hats

Stewardship Jack Series, Book 3

by Janice Mathews

Review&Herald®

REVIEW AND HERALD® PUBLISHING ASSOCIATION
SINCE 1861 | WWW.REVIEWANDHERALD.COM

Copyright © 2013 by Janice Matthews

Published by Review and Herald® Publishing Association, Hagerstown, MD 21741-1119

Review and Herald® titles may be purchased in bulk for educational, business, fund-raising, or sales promotional use. For information, e-mail SpecialMarkets@reviewandherald.com.

The Review and Herald® Publishing Association publishes biblically based materials for spiritual, physical, and mental growth and Christian discipleship.

Cover design by Ron Pride/Review and Herald® Design Center
Interior design by Emily Ford / Review and Herald® Design Center
Photos by Janice Mathews, Gary Eldridge (cover), Joseph Collins (pp. 6, 17), and Larry Blackmer (pp. 9, 21).

Sponsored by:
North American Division Stewardship Ministries
General Conference Stewardship Ministries
North American Division Children's Ministries
General Conference Children's Ministries

PRINTED IN U.S.A.

17 16 15 14 13   5 4 3 2 1

Library of Congress Cataloging-in-Publication Data
Mathews, Janice, 1954-   .
Jack's Hats / Janice Mathews.
p. cm. – (Stewardship Jack series; bk. 3)
1. Christian stewardship–Juvenile literature. 2. Jesus Christ–Parables–Juvenile literature. I. Title.
BV772.M3865 2012
248¹.6–dc23
                                    2012048271

ISBN 978-0-8280-2718-2

Introduction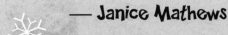

The Stewardship Jack series is a set of books for children, preschool through second grade, on the topic of stewardship. These books are presented in a whimsical manner, using Jack, a goldendoodle dog, who has become "Stewardship Jack."

The first three books are:

- Book 1, *Jack Gives Back* (stewardship of talents and faithful stewards)
- Book 2, *Jack and the 10 Rules* (Ten Commandments)
- Book 3, *Jack's Hats* (good and faithful stewards use their talents)

Plans are to have future books, designed to attract the attention of children to other important topics about stewardship, and to engender a positive regard for the care and use of the resources God has given. Let me introduce Stewardship Jack (who absolutely loves people):

Jack was the only one left from his litter.
It seemed no one wanted him, but he wasn't bitter.
God had a plan for him right from the start—
He helps me write books we hope will touch your heart.

— Janice Mathews

Stewardship Jack is a pup, black and furry;

He really can't talk, but gives "advice" to my query.

Sometimes his actions speak louder than words:

"We've all received talents, so be good stewards."

Christ tells a story in the book of Matthew–

Servants given talents, five, one, and two.

If they each faithfully managed what they were given,

Each would be blessed with joy from heaven.

We all have talents and things we can do.

Some have a lot, and some but a few.

We're to faithfully use them for Jesus each day,

Awaiting His coming and His "Well done" to say.

What gift do you have, what hat do you wear?
Jack tells us something that we need to hear.

**What hat is that, Jack?
Is that really you? Is that what you do?**

No, this is a cowboy's hat.

A cowboy rides horses and takes care of cattle.

I don't think I, Jack, could stay in the saddle.

What hat is that, Jack?
Is that really you? Is that what you do?

No, this is a baseball cap.

A baseball player bats, catches, and runs the bases.

I'd rather fetch sticks and run rabbit races.

What hat is that, Jack?
Is that really you? Is that what you do?

No, this is a sun visor.

A visor is worn by those who play tennis.

I could chase the ball, but I'd be more of a menace.

What hat is that, Jack?
Is that really you? Is that what you do?

No, this is a toboggan.

A toboggan is worn to keep ears warm in the cold.

I grow my own earmuffs and don't need it, I'm told.

Sun Screen

What hat is that, Jack?
Is that really you? Is that what you do?

No, this is a sun hat.

Sun hats protect girls' faces, you see.

But I'm a boy dog–how silly that would be.

What hat is that, Jack?
Is that really you? Is that what you do?

22

No, this is a nurse's cap.

Nurses are people who care for the sick.

I can't do that, but I could give them a lick.

What hat is that, Jack?
Is that really you? Is that what you do?

No, this is a hard hat.

A hard hat is worn by those in construction.

I hate to admit it, but I'm better at destruction.

25

What hat is that, Jack?
Is that really you? Is that what you do?

It's not a hat–it's my soft furry head.
I lay my head on one who will let me
So they can stroke and pat me gently.

No fancy hat–just being me.
It's amazing to see and curious to tell
How it seems to make sadness gone for a spell.

That is my hat. That's what I do.

I share what God gave me, and so can you.

Even if your talents seem small and of no account,

God can use them, no matter the amount.

God loves and encourages, but never forces.
Do what you can with your given resources.
He's coming soon, and there's much to do.
God gave you your hat, so do something too!

You're unique and special as a human, you know,

So put on your best hat before you go.